21st-Century
Engineering Solutions
for Climate Change

RISING SEA LEVELS

JOANNE MATTERN

Cavendish
Square

New York

Published in 2019 by Cavendish Square Publishing, LLC
243 5th Avenue, Suite 136, New York, NY 10016

Website: cavendishsq.com

This publication represents the opinions and views of the author based on his or her personal
experience, knowledge, and research. The information in this book serves as a general
guide only. The author and publisher have used their best efforts in preparing this book and
disclaim liability rising directly or indirectly from the use and application of this book.

All websites were available and accurate when this book was sent to press.

Library of Congress Cataloging-in-Publication Data

Names: Mattern, Joanne, 1963- author.
Title: Rising sea levels / Joanne Mattern.
Description: New York : Cavendish Square, 2019. | Series: 21st-century engineering solutions
for climate change | Includes bibliographical references and index. | Audience: Grades 7-12.
Identifiers: LCCN 2017049198 (print) | LCCN 2017054809 (ebook) |
ISBN 9781502638298 (library bound) | ISBN 9781502638304 (pbk.) | ISBN 9781502638311 (ebook)
Subjects: LCSH: Shore protection--Juvenile literature. | Sea level--Juvenile literature.
Classification: LCC TC330 (ebook) | LCC TC330 .M285 2019 (print) | DDC 627/.58--dc23
LC record available at https://lccn.loc.gov/2017049198

Editorial Director: David McNamara
Editor: Kristen Susienka
Copy Editor: Rebecca Rohan
Associate Art Director: Amy Greenan
Designer: Alan Sliwinski/Megan Mette
Production Coordinator: Karol Szymczuk
Photo Research: J8 Media

The photographs in this book are used by permission and through the courtesy of:
Cover, p. 1 Curioso/Shutterstock.com; p. 4 Sinan Hussain/AP Photo; p. 8 eppicphotography/iStock;
p. 9 Carsten Peter/National Geographic/Getty Images; p. 11 Dan Bach Kristensen/Shutterstock.
com; p. 14 Julie Dermansky/Corbis News/Getty Images; p. 16 Image Source/Getty Images; p. 19
Jan Tove Johansson/The Image Bank/Getty Images; p. 21 Anders Peter Photography/Shutterstock.
com; p. 22 Jesse Allen/NASA Earth Observatory/Wikimeida Commons/File:Arctic Sea Ice Minimum
Comparison.png/CC PD; p. 23 Wolfgang Kaehler/LightRocket/Getty Images; p. 25 Doug Perrine/
Photolibrary/Getty Images; p. 26 Andreas Weith/Wikimedia Commons/File:Endangered arctic
– starving polar bear.jpg/CC BY-SA 4.0; p. 27 AGF/Universal Images Group/Getty Images; p.
28 NASA/JPL; p. 29 Jonas Gratzer/LightRocket/Getty Images; p. 32 Laborant/Shutterstock.
com; p. 35 FLPA/Gary K Smith/Corbis Documentary/Getty Images; p. 40 John G. Manbanglo/
AFP/Getty Images; p. 45 Moorefam/iStock; p. 46 Douglas Sacha/Moment/Getty Images; p. 48
Brooks Kraft/Corbis Historical/Getty Images; p. 52 Mel Evans/AP Photo; p. 60 Mark Wilson/
Getty Images; p. 62 GLF Media/Shutterstock.com; p. 67 Vincenzo Pinto/AFP/Getty Images.

Printed in the United States of America

CONTENTS

CHAPTER ONE

WHY ARE SEA LEVELS RISING?

The people who live on the Maldives, a group of islands in the Indian Ocean, have a big problem. Their homes are disappearing. It's not just their houses that are in danger, but the entire island they live on is sinking into the sea. The Maldives are just a few feet above sea level, and sea levels have been rising for a number of years. The prospect of the entire

Opposite: A soldier rides through a flooded street in the Maldives. Rising sea levels have threatened this island nation with extinction.

island chain disappearing under the waves has led government officials to seriously consider relocating the entire population of three hundred thousand people to another country, such as India, Sri Lanka, or Australia.

The Maldives are not the only nation facing disaster from rising sea levels. Around the world, islands are seeing sea levels rise to dangerous heights. According to the Intergovernmental Panel on Climate Change, the most vulnerable nations are the Marshall Islands, Kiribati, Tuvalu, Tonga, the Federated States of Micronesia, the Cook Islands, Antigua and Nevis, and the Maldives. And NASA recently predicted that the world will see the oceans rise 3 feet (91 centimeters) or more by the end of the twenty-first century. For islands that are just 5 or 6 feet (152 to 183 cm) above sea level, this prediction is a death sentence.

A Warmer Planet

People who live on islands or along the coast are familiar with flooding. However, the first eighteen years of the twenty-first century have seen a dramatic increase in rising sea levels that goes beyond flooding from a bad storm. Floods are becoming more common, and entire landforms are threatened because of climate change.

Earth has warmed 1.4 degrees Fahrenheit (0.8 degrees Celsius) since 1880. That might not sound like much, but global warming has had a huge impact on our planet's climate and its sea levels. While it's true that the earth has always gone through cycles of warming and cooling, humans have had a great effect on this process. Human activities, such as burning coal and other fossil fuels, have accelerated the rate of global warming. Burning fossil fuels releases large amounts of gases into the atmosphere. Some of these gases trap heat. That trapped heat causes the planet's temperature to rise.

Humans have also cut down millions of acres of tropical forests. Eliminating forests also affects the earth's temperature. Think about the process of photosynthesis. It enables plants to make their own food. During this process, plants absorb carbon dioxide and release oxygen. However, the loss of forests means there are fewer trees to absorb carbon dioxide and other greenhouse gases. This

The brutal result of clear-cut logging can be seen in this photo of a destroyed forest.

has led to a large increase in the amount of carbon dioxide in the atmosphere, which has raised Earth's temperature. In addition, burning trees adds even more carbon dioxide to the air. Scientists estimate that 1.5 billion tons (1.4 billion metric tons) of carbon dioxide are added every year from cutting down and burning forests.

Global Warming and Sea Levels

Global warming doesn't just affect the temperature. It also affects sea levels. Rising temperatures warm ocean waters. The waters expand as the temperature increases. This process is called thermal expansion. About half of the planet's rise in sea level can be accounted for by warmer ocean water taking up more space.

Scientists have a number of ways of measuring the rise in global sea levels. Core samples, tide gauge readings, and most recently, satellite measurements tell us that over the past century, the Global Mean Sea Level (GMSL) has risen by 4 to 8 inches (10 to 20 cm). The rate has increased at an alarming speed

Scientists drill into an ice cave in Antarctica to retrieve a sample for study.

Projections for global sea level rise by the year 2100 range from 8 inches (20 cm) to 6.6 feet (201 cm) above 1992 levels.

in recent years. In 2014, the global sea level was 2.6 inches (6.6 cm) higher than it was in 1993.

Melting Ice

Another important effect of global warming is that it melts glaciers, ice caps, and ice sheets. Large ice formations, such as glaciers and ice caps (the ice present at the North and South Poles), naturally melt and shrink each summer as the temperature warms. They regain the lost ice in the winter as more snow and ice accumulate to balance out the loss from melting. However, higher temperatures in the late twentieth and early twenty-first centuries have caused more ice to melt during the summer and less ice to form during the winter. Also, warmer temperatures have caused less snow to fall during winters, and spring temperatures have arrived earlier than in the past. This imbalance has led to significant loss of ice and a significant gain in the amount of melting ice. It has also caused sea levels to rise. All that extra melting ice adds more water to Earth's oceans. As the rate of ice loss accelerated in the early 2000s, it accounted for 75 to 80 percent of the total increase in sea levels between 2003 and 2007.

The rise in temperature also causes the massive ice sheets that cover Greenland and Antarctica to melt quicker. Scientists believe that melting ice and

People are dwarfed by a huge melting glacier in Greenland.

rising seawater are seeping beneath Greenland and West Antarctica's ice sheets. The streams created from this process melt the ice and cause it to move more quickly into the sea. Likewise, it raises the water level. Higher sea temperatures, in addition, are causing the giant ice shelves that extend out from Antarctica to melt underneath. In time, the ice shelves weaken and break off into icebergs, causing more loss to the ice sheets and adding more water to the ocean.

What Are the Risks?

Rising sea levels bring risks to land in a number of ways. For one, rising sea levels cause waves to flow farther inland. This can create shoreline erosion, damaging landforms and putting nearby buildings

/ DID YOU KNOW? /

There is a difference between a glacier and an iceberg. A glacier is a large sheet of ice that moves very slowly. Icebergs are large pieces of ice that break off of glaciers, ice caps, and ice sheets. They float in the ocean until they melt.

and roads at risk of flooding. Salt water from the oceans can also flow into freshwater bays and seep into coastal groundwater. This rise in salt water can damage systems that provide freshwater for agriculture and public water supplies.

Rising sea levels also create increased damage during storms. Hurricanes often produce violent waves of water called storm surges. A storm surge is created by hurricane winds. These winds pull water away from the shore and pile it up in a huge wave. As the winds rotate and the hurricane draws nearer to land, water gets pushed back to shore. Violent storm surges caused a great deal of damage to neighborhoods along the East Coast of the United States during Hurricane Sandy in 2012.

Storm tides are another critical danger. They occur when a storm surge happens during high tide. The combination of higher tides and the extra volume and force of a storm surge can lead to tremendous damage.

And then there are those islands like the Maldives. In the twenty-first century, this nation is facing increased flooding and, eventually, complete loss because of rising tides. Like the Maldives, areas of low-

When Hurricane Sandy struck New Jersey's shore in October 2012, its power dragged this roller coaster out to sea.

lying coastal land are expected to be gradually covered by rising sea levels. This damaging rise won't just affect islands in faraway oceans. Scientists believe that a rise of 2 feet (61 cm) above today's sea level would put more than $1 trillion of property and structures in the United States at risk, including much of Florida and major cities such as New York. According to *National Geographic*, one scientific projection goes as far as saying that if Greenland's ice sheet melts completely, sea levels will rise high enough to swamp major cities around the world, even if they are not on the coast.

All of these climate changes have led to rising sea levels and created a serious problem for the world. It is a problem best faced before time runs out.

CLIMATE CHANGE SKEPTICS

Not everyone believes that climate change is something to be alarmed about. Skeptics state that climate change has been occurring for thousands of years and is a natural part of life on Earth. They do not believe that rising sea levels can be blamed on increased human activity. Their claims include: the climate has changed before; scientific models are unreliable; sea level rise is exaggerated; and evidence to support rising sea levels and global warming is just not accurate. These skeptics can find sources to support their arguments. However, most mainstream scientists and organizations have made it clear that Earth's temperature is rising as a result of human activity, and the planet's sea levels are rising as well.

CHAPTER TWO

A RISING PROBLEM

The twenty-first century is not the first or only time people have faced danger from rising water. However, as sea levels rise faster than ever, this has become a problem with many serious consequences.

Melting Ice Caps

One of the most alarming causes of rising sea levels is the melting of the polar ice caps. Ice caps are large

Opposite: The sun rises over planet Earth. Because of Earth's shape, sunlight hits different parts of the planet with different intensities.

areas of land at the North and South Poles. Without climate change activity, the poles are permanently covered with ice.

Ice caps form because of the angle at which sunlight hits the earth. At the equator, sunlight hits at a 90-degree angle, which creates an abundant and steady temperature and amount of sunlight. However, because Earth is round, sunlight strikes the poles at a more indirect angle than it does at the equator. The sunlight at the equator is spread out over a larger area. The indirect angle at the poles means they receive less solar energy, so temperatures are colder.

About 90 percent of the world's ice is locked up in the continent of Antarctica, which covers the South Pole. The ice that covers Antarctica is an average of 7,000 feet (2,133 meters) thick. If all of that ice melted, the world's oceans would rise an estimated 200 feet (61 m)! However, the temperature in Antarctica is well below freezing all year long, even with global warming.

The ice in the Arctic, including the North Pole, also covers the part of Canada that lies above the Arctic Circle. Canada's Arctic region is covered by approximately 7,660 square miles (19,839 sq km) of land ice. Although this is much less than the ice covering Antarctica and Greenland, which measures 5.2 million square miles (13.4 million sq km) in Antarctica and 650,000 square miles (1.6 million sq km) in Greenland, Canada's ice is still quite significant.

Just a few decades ago, the ice covering the North Pole was 10 to 12 feet (3 to 3.6 m) thick. Some areas of the Arctic were covered in ice 150 feet (46 m) deep. That ice is long gone. Some estimates put the

Water pours from a melting glacier and drains into the sea.

A Rising Problem

total volume of Arctic sea ice at 75 percent less than it was fifty years ago.

In the next one hundred years, melting glaciers and ice caps in the Arctic could cause global sea levels to rise by 8 to 16 inches (20 to 40 cm). While this rise does not sound like much, it would have a devastating effect on coastlines around the world.

Greenland in Trouble

Another huge concern for scientists is the amount of land ice melting in Greenland. Contrary to its name, Greenland is not very green. It is also closer to the equator than Antarctica, which means temperatures are warmer in Greenland. Warmer temperatures lead to more ice melt. Scientists estimate that if all of Greenland's ice melted, it would raise the ocean about 20 feet (6 m).

The rise in water and air temperature at the poles has had a huge effect on Greenland's ice cap. Until the 1980s, Greenland's ice never experienced significant melting during the summer. However, by 2012, 97 percent of the island's ice sheet had experienced surface melting. Greenland's melting ice is now the

A group of icebergs floats past Greenland's shore. Icebergs are huge chunks of ice that have broken off glaciers.

single largest contributor to the rise in global sea levels. Its melting ice cap adds approximately 72 cubic miles (300 cubic kilometers) of water to the ocean every year.

Minimums and Maximums

When measuring Arctic ice, scientists talk about sea ice minimum and sea ice maximum. The Arctic sea ice minimum marks the time of year when the sea ice is at its lowest. Typically, it occurs at the end of the summer melting season; however, in recent years, it has been occurring later because the melting season has been getting longer. The Arctic sea ice maximum is the day when Arctic sea ice is the largest

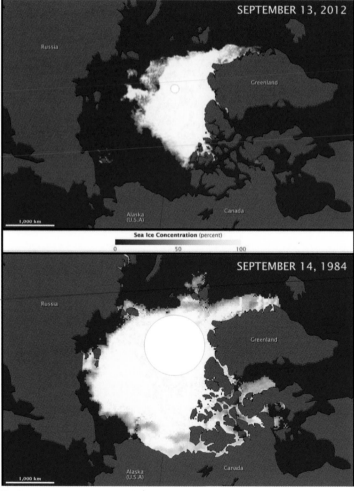

These charts show the drastic reduction of Arctic sea ice between September 1984 (*bottom*) and September 2012 (*top*).

and thickest. It usually takes place at the end of the winter cold season.

Scientists monitor winter sea ice in order to understand the state of the ice. In recent years, scientists have discovered that Arctic ice has not thickened or expanded as much during the winter cold season as in years past. This means that when the summer melting season arrives, the ice is now thinner and weaker. This, in turn, leads to more ice melting during the summer, creating a cycle that results in more ice loss every year.

Some scientists believe that the Arctic will be ice-free during the summer months as early as

Melting ice near Norway shows the effect of global warming.

A Rising Problem

2020. Others have said 2040 is a more likely date. This loss of ice will accelerate rising temperatures. Rising temperatures will, in turn, speed up the rise in sea levels.

Temperatures in the Arctic are rising twice as fast as they are anywhere else on Earth. Along with rising temperatures, scientists believe a possible cause for this loss of ice is the temperature of ocean water. In 2015, the temperature of the Arctic Ocean was about 33.63°F (0.9°C), a rise of a full degree Fahrenheit since 2000. Warmer ocean water creates a warmer air mass above the water. This warmer air mass spreads over the land and drives up temperatures there as well. It also warms the water flowing into the ocean from rivers and streams, which in turn makes the ocean even warmer.

Effects on Animals, Plants, and People

Melting ice caps don't just affect the water level. They affect plants, animals, and their habitats as well. All of the water stored in the ice caps is freshwater, while ocean water is salty. As the polar ice caps melt, they release freshwater in the ocean. This makes the ocean

Creatures such as this deep sea angler fish will be threatened if melting ice adds more freshwater to the saltwater oceans.

less salty. Plants and animals that are ocean dwellers have adapted to living in a salty habitat. If the habitat changes to more freshwater, animals and plants may not be able to survive in this new condition.

Although the ice caps are covered with ice and snow all year round, they are still home to many different living creatures. Many small plants, invertebrates (animals without backbones), and mammals live on or around the polar ice caps and depend on them for food and shelter. As the ice caps melt, these animals will be unable to find food, and they will lose their homes as well. In some areas of

Extensive ice melt in the Arctic has led to reduced food supply for polar bears. This wandering bear clearly shows the effects of starvation.

the Arctic, starving polar bears have been moving close to human villages and towns in search of food. This puts both animals and people at risk.

The effects of melting polar ice caps will affect areas of Earth far from the poles themselves. Without the ice caps, Earth's temperature will rise even more. This will lead to higher temperatures, which could have a huge impact on agriculture. One of the effects could be changing growing seasons, making it more difficult to grow crops in certain places. In addition, the loss of habitats causes animals to move to new areas. This can mean a lack of food for hunters and fishers in areas all over the world.

Ocean and Climate

Plants, animals, and people are not the only ones affected by rising sea levels and melting ice caps. The

An Inuit native fishes through the ice in Canada. These native people's traditional hunting methods are threatened by rising sea levels and global warming.

A Rising Problem

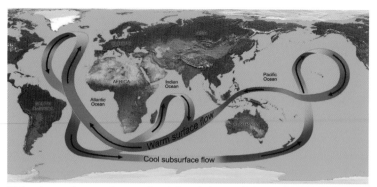

This chart shows the path of the Atlantic Meridional Overturning Circulation and how it affects weather around the world.

ocean and the atmosphere itself are also affected. Scientists believe that as ice caps melt and release more water into the oceans, they will disrupt a major circulation system called the Atlantic Meridional Overturning Circulation (AMOC). AMOC carries warm ocean water northward and, among other things, creates Europe's mild climate. Many climate models predict rising temperatures and rising sea levels could slow AMOC by 25 percent by 2100. A slower AMOC could change Europe's climate, but also affect weather and climate patterns around the world. This, in turn, will affect melting sea ice, creating another cycle that disrupts the planet.

The loss of sea ice and global warming will also affect the jet stream. The jet stream plays a major part in creating weather and climate conditions across the planet. It moves areas of warm and cool air around the globe and also moves weather systems around Earth. A loss of sea ice will change atmospheric pressure as well as the course of the jet stream. This change could bring colder Arctic air into the middle part

A woman wades through floodwaters outside her home in Kiribati, an island nation that faces certain destruction from rising sea levels.

A Rising Problem

of the earth and affect storm patterns throughout the world.

Disappearing Nations

The people who live on small or low-lying islands face a real danger from rising water. In nations such as the United States, people who live along the coast usually can leave and go inland if their homes flood. They might not want to leave, but it is at least an option. People who live on small islands, on the other hand, do not have the choice of moving inland. That is because inland areas tend to flood as much as coastal areas. For many, the only options people have are to leave their island homes and move far away, or stay where they are and ride out the storm.

The island nation of Kiribati is made up of thirty-three coral atolls and reef islands in the Pacific Ocean. The islands are about 6 feet (1.8 m) above sea level, putting the entire nation at risk of flooding. Already, rising tides cause numerous floods and have not only contaminated the nation's water supply but damaged its food supply. Scientists predict that Kiribati will be

FLOODING: AN ANCIENT PROBLEM

While the effects of rising sea levels have increased during the twenty-first century, coastal flooding has always been a problem. Such evidence of flooding affecting ancient communities was discovered in 2012. That year, a Native American burial ground in Cedar Key, Florida, was threatened by floodwaters. Archaeologists hurried to save bones and other artifacts from the area before it disappeared into the Gulf of Mexico. During their dig, they made a surprising discovery. The burial ground was actually a *re*burial ground. That meant that the skeletons there had initially been buried elsewhere. They had then been moved to the current location. Why? The archaeologists believe that the ancient people had to move because of rising water, and they made sure to take everything—even their buried ancestors—with them.

uninhabitable by 2100. Parts of the islands will be lost by 2050.

There is no stopping the rising sea, so Kiribati's government has taken action to move to higher and safer ground. In 2014, the nation bought 6,000 acres (2,428 hectares) of land on the island of Fiji, about 1,000 miles (1,609 km) away and at a higher elevation. Kiribati's 110,000 residents have been urged to

The trees in this field are suffering from the ill effects of flooding, which washes away soil and damages roots.

"migrate with dignity" and start new lives on Fiji. Anote Tong, then-president of Kiribati, said the land purchase was not only a practical response to the crisis, but it was also a cry for attention. He wanted the rest of the world to know what rising sea levels were doing to his home.

Salty Contamination

Rising sea levels impact cities and nations in more ways than just covering land. There are many other serious consequences, such as saltwater contamination and loss of crops.

As seawater flows farther onto the shore, it seeps into the freshwater sources in the ground. Many coastal areas rely on groundwater for their drinking water. Salt water is not only unsafe to drink, but the salt can ruin equipment used to process drinking water. While it is possible to remove the salt from water, desalination is an expensive and complicated process. Some communities are already investing in desalination plants to prepare for what could lie in store for them. However, the high cost of such plants makes it unlikely to be an option considered by every city on Earth.

Losing freshwater resources will also have a negative impact on farming. Agriculture relies on sources of freshwater, and crops can be killed or damaged by salt. If freshwater sources are contaminated by salt water, acres of farmland could be lost.

DID YOU KNOW?

According to an article in *National Geographic*, sea levels are rising by about 0.13 inches (3.3 millimeters) every year.

These sand dunes in England were damaged by a tidal surge in 2013.

Harming Plants and Animals

As salt water floods coastal areas, it will also change the habitats where plants and animals live. Plants are extremely sensitive to the soil, water, and air that make up their environment. Adding salt water will change the chemical composition of the soil and make it impossible for some plants to survive. The scientific research organization Climate Central has reported that trees will be the most affected by a rise in salt water. They point out that trees have to work harder to pull water out of salty soil, and the extra effort can stunt their growth. Stunted or dying trees are common signs of sea level rise. Climate Central also notes that even trees that can grow in salty water are harmed by repeated flooding.

Animals are also harmed by sea-level rise. Many animals live on beaches and other coastal areas. As sea levels rise, these animals will lose their homes to flooding. Along with shelter, they may also lose sources of food. Shorebirds and sea turtles face additional danger, as floodwaters will wash away their nests.

Economic Concerns

Rising sea levels could have a big effect on property values. Homes and businesses on the water have always been seen as desirable. They have nice views of the ocean and access to beaches. They also cost a lot of money. However, as sea levels rise, many waterfront

ANCIENT BEATS MODERN

Today, we use concrete to build seawalls to hold back the ocean. However, these concrete walls need repair after a few decades because salt water is so damaging. The ancient Romans also needed to hold back the sea, and they used concrete too. However, their structures have lasted for more than two thousand years!

The ancient Romans mixed volcanic ash and quicklime to make a substance that actually grows stronger when it is exposed to salty water. Philip Brune, a researcher at DuPont and an expert in ancient Roman monuments, called the material "the most durable in human history."

Is the ancient Roman recipe for concrete something we could use today? Scientists are trying to find out by creating their own similar concrete from volcanic rocks.

areas could be flooded, and homes and businesses could be destroyed. The real estate industry worries that potential buyers will not want to buy homes on the water for fear that rising sea levels will place them squarely in a flood zone. Any flooding that might occur at these places could be very expensive to fix.

The tourism industry would also be hit hard by a rise in sea level. Many beaches, waterfront parks, and other attractions would be ruined when sea levels rise. Losing these attractions means that tourists will take their business somewhere safer and on higher ground. Many communities on the coast rely on tourists to help them make a living. Tourists visit local shops, cafés, and attractions. Losing waterfront attractions could be an economic deathblow to these areas.

A Homeless Population

If the ocean rises to dangerous levels, tourists aren't the only ones who will be staying away from coastal areas. The people who live there will also lose their homes. Climate Central estimates that up to 760 million people around the world could become homeless because of rising sea levels. They project that if global temperatures rise by 7.2°F (4°C), sea levels will rise by 35 feet (10.7 m). That would submerge the homes of 10 percent of the world's population.

Many major coastal cities are threatened by sea rise. Throughout history, cities have been founded near water to take advantage of easy trade and transportation routes. The East and West Coasts of the United States are lined with major cities. Key cities in Asia, Australia, and Europe are also located along coasts. Some of these cities are in low-lying coastal areas. In China and the United States alone, more than 170 million people live in such regions. As sea levels rise, these areas will be under water. The challenge to scientists and engineers is how to stop the danger.

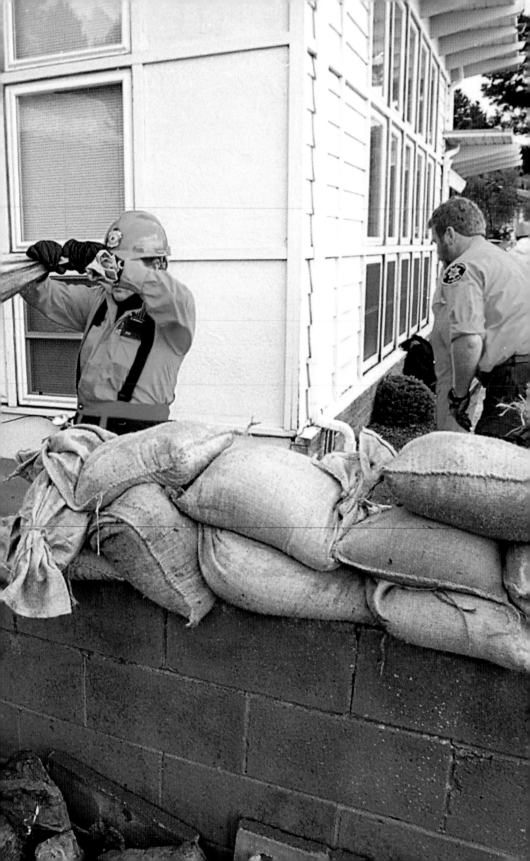

CHAPTER THREE

MODERN SOLUTIONS AND INNOVATIONS

With many scientists predicting an 18-inch (46 cm) rise in sea levels by the year 2100, humans can no longer sit back and wait. Many scientists believe it is too late to stop the rise in sea levels. Instead, people must work to protect their land from the sea and find ways to live with rising sea levels. It's time for cities around the world to take action. Over the

Opposite: Workers carry sandbags to protect homes in a flooded area in California.

past few years, many scientists and engineers have been working to create new technologies to keep the water back.

Holding Back the Sea

People have benefited from living along the sea ever since civilization began. For one, it is an excellent source of food. It also provides easy access to transportation across the water. Easy transportation, in turn, allows industry to flourish. It also provides routes for countries to trade with other nations. Land on the coast has always been valuable. Real estate values for properties near water are usually higher than for properties farther inland. In addition, beaches provide a source of recreation and beauty that can make an area more desirable to live in.

However, living by the sea also has its dangers. Waves are constantly creeping up the beach or pounding against the rocks. The movement of water on the shore can lead to erosion. In time, the sea claims more and more land, putting beachfront property and sometimes entire communities at risk. When a storm strikes, there is even more danger as the sea rises onto the land, flooding houses, businesses, and roads. As sea levels rise, the risk to coastal communities rises with them.

For thousands of years, ever since the days of the ancient Romans, coastal communities have relied on seawalls to prevent flooding. A seawall is usually a large cement structure built along the shoreline to prevent water from flowing onto the land. Seawalls are meant to stop shoreline erosion and also stop flooding, especially from storm surges.

Benefits and Drawbacks of Seawalls

Seawalls are often the first line of defense in protecting coastal communities. While they are not perfect, studies show that they do work. In 2016, a team of scientists from universities in the United States and Japan compared the loss of life in Japan during major tsunamis in 1896, 1933, 1960, and 2011. The study indicated that seawalls 30 feet (9.1 m) high were best, reducing destruction by up to 6 percent.

Although they offer protection, seawalls also have their drawbacks. One of the most significant drawbacks is a seawall's effect on the environment it is built to protect. When a seawall is built, it changes the beach's structure and environment. Putting up a wall means the sand behind the wall will no longer wash away because of erosion. However, things are quite different on the other side of the wall. As waves strike the seawall and move back into the ocean, they remove sand from the beach. In time, the beach in front of the wall is completely lost to erosion and the sea is closer to land.

Building a seawall also divides an ecosystem. Animals and plants that once lived together on the beach are now separated from each other. Part of the beach is also unable to be accessed by people who visit the beach. This can lead to overcrowding and overuse of the remaining beach. These side effects can damage the area and cause more habitat loss. In addition, seawalls are usually not designed to look good. Their appearance can remove some of the beach's natural beauty.

Finally, seawalls are under constant attack from the sea. The pounding of salty waves against the wall damages it. Cracks and holes form that allow

Constant, crashing waves have damaged this seawall along the coast in England.

seawater to flow past the wall. Ocean water can also flow under the seawall. This eventually causes the wall to fail. In a bad storm, a damaged seawall can collapse and create serious flooding.

Other Engineering Techniques

In addition to seawalls, engineers have invented other ways to protect coastal land. Groynes are low-lying wooden walls that extend out into the sea. Groynes are not as tall or as thick as seawalls. Their purpose is to capture sand that is washed down the beach and hold it in place. In time, this technique creates a new beach and increases the distance waves have to travel to reach land. This extra distance also makes the waves weaker when they finally reach shore. However, groynes are only useful under specific conditions. They also do not work on all beaches.

Breakwaters are another technique meant to lessen the impact of waves on the shoreline. Breakwaters are concrete walls built offshore. They extend into the body of water. However, these walls are unattractive and are easily damaged during storms.

Some techniques are specifically designed to lessen the impact of waves against cliffs. This is

A gabion wall is one way to protect land from tidal erosion.

important because the impact of waves over time can erode cliffs, especially if they are made of a soft rock such as sandstone. In time, eroded cliffs will collapse, threatening the land and structures above them.

Revetments are a type of seawall built along the base of a cliff. They can be made of concrete or wood. They are built at an angle and can have a rippled surface. This surface lessens the force of incoming waves. These structures are useful for stopping coastal erosion, but they are expensive to build.

Rocks are often used to protect cliffs from erosion. Gabions are rocks wrapped in metal mesh and placed at the base of cliffs. They lessen the force of the water and prevent the sea from damaging the cliff. Riprap is a simpler form that includes rocks placed against the base of a cliff. However, gabions and riprap can be washed away by the waves and are not particularly good at stopping rising waters.

Soft Engineering Techniques

New technology can create solutions to the problem of rising sea levels. However, some people have a different idea. Many organizations are looking at more natural solutions to stop the damage caused by the rising seas.

Using seawalls and other human-made structures is known as hard engineering. Another technique is called soft engineering. Soft engineering uses natural elements to combat rising sea levels.

Many coastal communities add sand to beaches in a process called beach nourishment. This is often done after storms have caused beach erosion. Adding sand restores the beach and makes it wider. This

A tractor dumps fresh sand on a beach in Florida to restore dunes that were damaged by the Atlantic Ocean.

SEA LEVEL SOLUTIONS

A program at Florida International University is looking for ways to change urban landscapes to withstand flooding. The Sea Level Solutions Center was launched in 2015 as a way to help people understand, adapt, and persevere in the face of rising sea levels by focusing on the science behind the rising seas. The center has already made suggestions to improve drainage and flood control in low-lying neighborhoods in Miami and is working with local governments, scientists, private corporations, and universities to combine knowledge and invent solutions that will work in the real world.

means seawater has farther to travel, making it harder to reach structures on land and also reducing the force of waves as they hit the land. Sand dunes can also be created and kept off-limits to people who use the beach. This allows the sand to create a natural defense against the sea.

Some communities use plants to create an obstacle to the sea. A process called beach stabilization involves placing dead trees in the sand to keep the sand in place and create an area where the force of the waves can be absorbed without washing away the beach. Other communities have allowed small plants to grow along the coastline, turning part of the beach into a marsh. A marsh slows and absorbs the flow of water, which lessens the impact on the rest of the beach.

Living Shorelines

Dams and seawalls might not always be the best way to hold back the water. Japan, an island nation that is prone to tsunamis and flooding, also uses a natural way to control the sea. Coastal forests along the shoreline have been proven to reduce destruction from flooding. This is an example of a promising concept called living shorelines.

A living shoreline uses plants, rocks, reefs, and other natural, native material to create a barrier between the water and the land. Some living shorelines only use vegetation as a buffer. Others combine soft materials, such as plants, with hard materials, such as coral reefs, rocks, or wood. This is a different approach from artificial, or hard, shoreline structures, such as walls, bulkheads, or dams.

Living shorelines create a buffer from waves. This buffer can reduce the force of waves and lower damage from erosion. Living shorelines can also help land hold its shape and prevent it from washing away. Features such as marshes and coral reefs act as natural barriers to waves. Fifteen feet (4.6 m) of marsh can absorb 50 percent of wave energy. Natural shorelines also trap sediment from tidal waters. This can add soil to the coastline and counter the effects of erosion.

Living shorelines benefit coastal communities in other ways. Adding plant life can improve the environment by reducing the amount of carbon in the air. Just 1 square mile (2.6 square kilometers) of salt marsh can store the carbon equivalent of 76,000 gallons (287,691 liters) of gas every year.

In addition, living shorelines can benefit animals. While seawalls can cut off migration routes and change habitats so that animals can no longer thrive there, natural shorelines add resources, improve water and soil quality, and create habitats that can increase biodiversity. People can also benefit from the creation of new recreation areas or parks.

Meadowlands

A large swampy area in New Jersey known as the Meadowlands suffered severe flooding from

This barrier wall in New Jersey's Meadowlands was no match for Hurricane Sandy in 2012. The storm created a tidal surge that damaged more than two thousand homes and buildings.

Hurricane Sandy's storm surge in 2012. Because of poor planning and overdevelopment, the waters that rushed into the Meadowlands had nowhere to go. The result was widespread flooding and property damage in many communities. Architects from the Netherlands partnered with scientists from the Massachusetts Institute of Technology's Center for Advanced Urbanization to propose a more natural landscape called the New Meadowlands.

Features of the New Meadowlands combine marshes and a system of raised banks called berms to create flood resistance with recreational benefits. Restored wetlands between the outer berm and the sea would soak up seawater and slow down tidal waves. The area would also serve as a wildlife refuge. An inner berm would protect ditches and ponds that could hold rainwater and prevent it from flooding local streets and storm drains. The plan includes a large recreation zone, and even bike lanes and a bus lane across the top of the berms. The goal is to work with nature rather than viewing it as a threat, and create an urban development that is more livable and able to adapt to a changing environment.

New Innovations

Living shorelines are an important weapon in the fight against rising sea levels, but they are not always the best option. Different solutions are needed, especially in coastal cities that face dangerous flooding. Areas around the world are inventing new ideas that might make it possible for coastal cities to survive in a world of rising waters.

The Golden Gate Barrage

The residents of San Francisco have reason to worry about rising sea levels. The city sits on the end of a peninsula and is surrounded by the Pacific Ocean and the San Francisco Bay. It hosts many large and well-known companies and is one of the most expensive places to live in the United States.

Many technology companies and city officials are looking into a system that would protect San Francisco from rising waters. One of the most ambitious plans is called the Golden Gate Barrage. A barrage is a barrier across a waterway. The Golden Gate Barrage would be a complex system of dams, locks, and pumps that would be built across the San Francisco Bay, near the Golden Gate Bridge. In theory, the barrage would work because there is only one way for water to flow in and out of the bay.

The main feature of the Golden Gate Barrage would be a 2-mile (3.2 km), 500-foot (152 m) wall built across the San Francisco Bay. Because just putting up a wall would be too disruptive to ship traffic and marine life, and because it would change the chemistry of the water in the bay, the barrage would have to include many features to solve these problems. Locks would have to be built to allow ship traffic to pass in and out of the bay. Pumps would transfer ocean water in and out of the bay as well.

Not everyone is a fan of the Golden Gate Barrage. In a 2007 study—the last time the project was seriously considered—investigators pointed out that if the barrage failed, the entire bay area would flood. In addition, the 2007 study found that building the barrage would have severe and negative consequences on marine life, animal migration, sediment deposits, and the health of wetlands in the bay area. Engineers believe a better system that has different points of protection would be a safer option.

The biggest problem facing the project is the cost. The only comparable project was the Three Gorges Dam built in China in the early 2000s to control flooding on the Yangtze River. This project cost $15 billion. The Golden Gate Barrage would be larger and more complicated than the Three Gorges Dam, so the cost would be much higher.

So far, no progress has been made in actually building the Golden Gate Barrage. If seriously considered again, the project would be the most expensive and complicated civil engineering project in history. However, it may be necessary to save the "City by the Bay" from destruction.

A Different Idea

In 2008, the San Francisco architecture firm Kuth Ranieri proposed a different plan to manage the water levels in San Francisco Bay. This plan is called Folding Waters. It would entail building fifteen levees around San Francisco Bay. These levees would protect the area without putting all the efforts in one single structure that could be damaged or destroyed. The tops of the levees would have winglike structures that could swing out when the tide rose. This action would create waterfalls that would flow into a gutter. That water could then be pumped out of the bay and back into the ocean. Pumps in the walls could create tides that would protect and nourish marine ecosystems in the bay.

Like the Golden Gate Barrage, building Folding Waters would be mind-bogglingly expensive and complicated. No one knows if simpler plans, such as traditional dams or seawalls, living shorelines, or controlled flooding, would be effective. It is also unclear who would pay for such a huge engineering project.

Solutions for the Metropolis

In 2012, large areas of New York City flooded following a storm surge caused by Hurricane Sandy. After the storm, Mayor Michael Bloomberg proposed a $20 billion plan to protect the city using a complex system of levees, seawalls, floodgates, breakwaters, and wetlands. In the years that followed, no real action has taken place to make Bloomberg's plans a reality. However, it is clear that a metropolitan area with such a huge population has to make some plans to survive the rise in sea levels—or at least the next powerful storm.

In 2017, an organization called Regional Plan Association created a long-range plan. It explored ideas to protect the New York metropolitan area—which includes 2.5 million people in New York and New Jersey who currently live in designated flood zones—from rising sea levels over the next fifty years. Their report, called *A Region Transformed*, set out unusual and innovative plans for the area. The plan's motto is "receive, protect, adapt," and it shows a region adapting to climate change and the rising sea levels it will bring. Homes and recreation areas could even be built on docks in flooded areas, creating a floating city.

A Region Transformed lays out a dynamic plan that preserves parts of the city by allowing water to reclaim lower-lying areas. Neighborhoods on higher ground would be prepared to house larger numbers of people, while low-lying areas would be allowed to return to nature. Flooded areas could become new parks or even coastal energy farms.

Other Cities, Other Ideas

In Boston, another low-lying city, a commission appointed by the mayor proposed that people and companies who owned waterfront properties should build seawalls and other barriers to protect themselves from future storms. Other politicians have called for a series of dams and locks to surround the city. However, as in New York City, nothing has been done to put any plans into action.

In 1900, the island city of Galveston, Texas, was wiped out by a powerful hurricane. Between 6,000 and 12,000 people died and more than 3,600 buildings were destroyed. It was the deadliest natural disaster in US history. Today, almost 50,000 people live in Galveston. Scientists predict that the city would lose

/ DID YOU KNOW? /

Dams and gates work by redistributing the flow of water. A dam blocks the flow entirely. Gates in the dam can be opened and closed to control how much water is behind the dam and how much water flows downstream.

Manhattan is one city that may be affected by rising sea levels in the future.

10 percent of its land if sea levels rose by 3 feet (0.9 m), and more than 50 percent of its land if sea levels rise by 4 feet (1.2 m).

Today, the city is studying a system of levees and gates. The project is nicknamed the "Ike Dike" after Hurricane Ike, whose storm surge caused massive flooding damage in Galveston in 2008.

Thinking Outside the Dam

Projects such as those under consideration in San Francisco, New York, Boston, and Galveston are complicated and rely on the latest technology. But they are really old-fashioned ways of blocking rising water and protecting land. Other cities and nations around the world are taking a more innovative approach to the problem of rising sea levels. For these cities, just building a dam is not good enough.

The Maeslant Barrier

The Netherlands is in constant danger from the sea. In 1953, a huge flood in the North Sea killed 1,835 people, left 70,000 people homeless, and caused millions of dollars in damages. After the tragedy, the government started building dams, dikes, levees, and storm-surge barriers to protect the nation from flooding.

About 20 percent of its land and 21 percent of its population are below sea level. To combat this problem, a series of dikes and other sea barriers has protected the country for many years. In addition, about 50 percent of the Netherlands lies less than 3 feet (0.9 m) above sea level. Since so much of its land is at risk from flooding, the government of the Netherlands has made flood control an important issue. A system called the Delta Works includes

The Netherlands' Maeslant Barrier gates are usually open to allow ship traffic, but they can be closed if a storm surge approaches.

embankments, dikes, and gates along areas where flooding occurs during storms.

The Delta Works began in the 1950s. Additional projects were added later. Originally, authorities wanted to keep the sea around the Netherlands' city of Rotterdam open. At that time, Rotterdam was the world's largest port and an important part of the Netherlands' economy. However, the dikes that were originally planned were not enough to protect Rotterdam's population. A new plan was put in place to build a moveable storm surge barrier to protect the area.

In 1991, the Netherlands began building its new weapon. That weapon was called the Maeslantkering, or Maeslant Barrier. The Maeslantkering is a movable storm surge. It provides a barrier across the New Waterway canal. It bridges the Rhine River and the North Sea.

The Maeslantkering is an amazing feat of engineering that defends Rotterdam from incoming seawater. The Maeslantkering is a set of two swinging doors. They are almost as long as the Eiffel Tower, creating the largest moving storm-surge barrier in the world. The doors are 689 feet (210 m) long and 72 feet (22 m) high. They move by way of a ball-and-socket mechanism mounted on both banks across the water. These huge doors are actually giant pontoons that can be filled with water. This ability is the secret to the Maeslantkering's success.

Normally, the Maeslantkering's doors are fully opened, providing a passage for ships to go through. However, when a storm surge of 9 feet (2.7 m) above normal sea level is predicted, the doors float toward each other. This closes the waterway. Then the doors' pontoons are filled with water. The additional weight makes them sink and turns the doors into a massive barrier. All these actions occur automatically, thanks to the Maeslantkering's computer system, which is linked to weather and sea level data.

It took just six years to build the Maeslantkering, which opened in 1997. Since then, a tidal surge has only caused the doors to close once, in 2007. The rest of the time, they stand ready to protect Rotterdam and its residents.

Saving a Sinking City

Venice, Italy, is another city that faces constant danger from rising water. The city is actually a series of 117 islands located in a lagoon. Its streets are canals, and for centuries, residents and visitors have used boats called gondolas to travel around the city. Venice's buildings stand on a foundation of sediment and wood.

At one time, the lagoon's waters protected the city from invading armies. But the water that makes Venice so unique and charming has turned into its biggest enemy. Between the 1920s and the 1970s, the city was constantly pumping water out of the lagoon. This caused the islands to sink, putting Venice

A SAFE WAY TO BUILD

Many bridges around the world float on pontoons. Why not use the same idea to float buildings and streets? Architect and inventor Greg Henderson and his colleagues at Arx Pax Labs are working on this idea to make flood-safe cities. The SAFE Foundation System is designed to float buildings, roads, and utilities in a few feet of water. The flotation system can adjust itself when the water rises, keeping buildings and infrastructure out of harm's way. Arx Pax is currently working on creating a SAFE Foundation System on the Pacific island of Kiribati, one of the world's most threatened places.

even more at risk. In the last century, Venice has sunk nearly 9 inches (23 cm).

On top of the sinking islands, Venice floods about one hundred times a year. These floods usually occur during the fall and winter. Add the problem of rising seas, and Venice may be doomed.

However, the city has taken steps to save itself. In 2003, a group of engineering companies began building the MOSE Project. MOSE is an acronym of the project's Italian name, which is Modulo Sperimentale Elettromeccanico. The MOSE Project installed underwater gates at the entrances of the three inlets where the waters of the Adriatic Sea enter Venice's lagoon. Sensors monitor the level of water at these entrances. When the sea rises too high, the sensors trigger a system that pumps air into the gates. The air forces the gates to rise and shut out the sea.

The first step of the MOSE Project was to install huge, 23,000-ton (20,865 metric ton) concrete foundations in the lagoon. Since then, a team of engineers has worked in a control center in the city, watching monitors and making calculations. Before the gates were installed, the people in the control

Technicians inspect the MOSE gates outside Venice, Italy, in 2014. Scientists hope the gates will reduce yearly floods in this watery city.

room conducted experiments, opening and closing imaginary gates to figure out exactly which gate should close at what time. The engineers created models for every possible situation.

The first gates of the MOSE Project were installed in 2015. Cameras are mounted on the 9-foot (2.7 m) gates and constantly send images and data to the control center so the engineers can monitor the water levels at all times. Data also includes information on wind speed and direction, the times of high and low tide, and other variables that can affect how fast the water will rise. If the water level rises more than 3.6 feet (1.1 m), the gates will swing into action. Engineers say that the project will not prevent all the flooding that occurs during the fall and winter of each year. However, it is hoped that major flooding events—perhaps seven each year—can be prevented or lessened.

Not an Easy Solution

The MOSE Project has the potential to protect Venice from drowning in rising sea levels, but it is a solution that creates other problems. Many scientists are concerned about the effects of blocking the inlets and changing the flow of water in the lagoon. Environmental activists have said that the biodiversity of the lagoon will be damaged. However, engineers have pointed out that the gates would only be closed for a few hours at a time during a storm, so they do not predict lasting damage to the environment.

Another concern is the cost, which was more than $7 billion. However, the cost of flood damage over the years is also quite large. Venice sees the high price as worth it if it will protect lives and property and save the city from destruction. Other people worry that the expensive system won't be able to stand up to sea levels that continue to rise. Is the MOSE Project throwing away a tremendous amount of money on something that might not work in the long run? No one knows, but it is the type of solution that more coastal communities have to consider.

The Ultimate Answer

Many people deny climate change and rising sea levels. Many more know the danger is real but feel powerless to do anything about it, or just don't think there are any answers. Although it may be too late to stop the rising tide of water around the world, it is not too late to look for solutions and put plans into action that will allow us to adapt to a changing world. There is no other choice if we want to live on a planet where the sea levels rise higher every year.

GLOSSARY

accelerate To get faster.

agriculture The science or practice of farming.

atmosphere The gases that surround Earth.

atoll A small island made of coral and surrounded by a lagoon.

berm A flat, raised piece of land along the water.

biodiversity The variety of life in an ecosystem.

desalination The process of removing salt from water.

elevation The height above sea level.

erosion The wearing away of soil or rock by water or wind.

gauge An instrument that measures something and shows the results in a visual display.

jet stream A strong air current that circles the globe several miles above Earth.

lagoon An area of salt water separated from the sea by a sandbank or reef.

levee An embankment meant to prevent an overflow of water.

lock A short section of a waterway where the water level can be changed to allow ships to move through.

marsh An area of low-lying land that is always wet.

pontoon A flat-bottomed cylinder that can be filled with water and is used to support a bridge or other structure.

skeptic A person who doubts accepted opinions.

FURTHER INFORMATION

Books

Blake, Kevin. *Rising Seas: Miami, Florida*. Eco-Disasters. New York: Bearport Publishing, 2017.

Buchanan, Shelly. *Global Warming*. Huntington Beach, CA: Teacher Created Materials, 2015.

Goodell, Jeff. *The Water Will Come: Rising Seas, Sinking Cities, and the Remaking of the Civilized World*. Boston, MA: Little, Brown & Company, 2017.

McPherson, Stephanie Sammartino. *Arctic Thaw: Climate Change and the Global Race for Energy Resources*. Minneapolis, MN: Twenty-First Century Books, 2015.

Sneideman, Joshua, and Erin Twamley. *Climate Change: Discover How It Impacts Spaceship Earth*. Build It Yourself. White River Junction, VT: Nomad Press, 2015.

Websites

The Kids Guide to Global Warming

http://www.kidzworld.com/article/17859-the-kids-guide-to-global-warming

This website for young students describes how global warming works, using diagrams and simple explanations.

NASA: Planet Health Report: Sea Level

https://climatekids.nasa.gov/health-report-sea-level

This website examines what happens to Earth if sea levels rise too quickly.

National Geographic: Sea Level Rise

http://www.nationalgeographic.com/environment/global-warming/sea-level-rise

This article describes sea level rise around the world.

Sea Level Rise

http://encyclopedia.kids.net.au/page/se/Sea_level_rise

This website explains sea level rise for young students.

SELECTED BIBLIOGRAPHY

"Causes of Sea Level Rise: What the Science Tells Us." Union of Concerned Scientists. http://www.ucsusa.org/global_warming/science_and_impacts/impacts/causes-of-sea-level-rise.html#.Wb_nDNFrzcs.

Clemens, Danny. DSCOVRD. "Climate Change by the Numbers: 760 Million Displaced by Rising Sea Levels." November 10, 2015. http://www.discovery.com/dscovrd/nature/climate-change-by-the-numbers-760-million-displaced-by-rising-sea-levels.

Cook, John. "Global Warming and Climate Change Myths." Skeptical Science. https://www.skepticalscience.com/argument.php.

Crugnale, James. "The Nine Most Endangered Islands in the World." Weather.com. February 18, 2016. https://weather.com/

science/environment/news/9-most-endangered-islands-in-the-world.

Denchak, Melissa. Natural Resources Defense Council. "Are the Effects of Global Warming Really That Bad?" March 15, 2016. https://www.nrdc.org/stories/are-effects-global-warming-really-bad.

"Five Reasons Why the Speed of Arctic Sea Ice Loss Matters." Carbon Brief. March 22, 2013. https://www.carbonbrief.org/five-reasons-why-the-speed-of-arctic-sea-ice-loss-matters.

Friedt, Sarah. "Polar Ice Caps: Temperature, Melting Effects & Facts." Study.com. http://study.com/academy/lesson/polar-ice-caps-temperature-melting-effects-facts.html.

Harvey, Chelsea. *Business Insider.* "Sea-Level Rise Will Cause More Than Flooding—These 5 Other Impacts of Rising Oceans Are Just As Bad." February 17, 2015. http://www.

businessinsider.com/5-terrifying-impacts-of-rising-sea-levels-2015-2.

Ives, Mike. "A Remote Pacific Nation, Threatened by Rising Seas." *New York Times*. July 2, 2016. https://www.nytimes.com/2016/07/03/world/asia/climate-change-kiribati.html?mcubz=0.

Kaushik. "The Netherland's Impressive Storm Surge Barriers." Amusing Planet. http://www.amusingplanet.com/2014/04/the-netherlands-impressive-storm-surge.html.

Knight, Sophie. "What Would an Entirely Flood-Proof City Look Like?" *Guardian*. September 25, 2017. https://www.theguardian.com/cities/2017/sep/25/what-flood-proof-city-china-dhaka-houston.

Lorentz, Katie. "Canada's Shrinking Ice Caps." NASA. March 4, 2005. https://www.nasa.gov/centers/langley/science/Canada_Ice.html.

NOAA. "Living Shorelines." https://www.habitatblueprint.noaa.gov/living-shorelines.

Pierre-Louis, Kendra. "What's Really Going On with Sea Level Rise?" *Popular Science*. http://www.popsci.com/nasa-data-sea-level-rise-decline-climate-change.

Regional Plan Association. "Coastal Urbanism." https://4c.rpa.org/corridors/coast.

Roush, Wade. "Sea Level Rise: Time for a Barrage of New Ideas." Xconomy. August 30, 2013. http://www.xconomy.com/national/2013/08/30/sea-level-rise-time-for-a-barrage-of-new-ideas/#.

Wadhams, Peter. "The Global Impacts of Rapidly Disappearing Sea Ice." Yale Environment 360. September 26, 2016. http://e360.yale.edu/features/as_arctic_ocean_ice_disappears_global_climate_impacts_intensify_wadhams.

Windsor, Antonia. "Inside Venice's Bid to Hold Back the Tide." *Guardian*. June 16, 2015. https://www.theguardian.com/cities/2015/jun/16/inside-venice-bid-hold-back-tide-sea-level-rise.

INDEX

ABOUT THE AUTHOR

Joanne Mattern has written more than 250 nonfiction books for young readers. She specializes in science, the environment, engineering, and history. Mattern has worked in the publishing field for more than twenty-five years and enjoys sharing information with young readers. She lives in New York State with her husband, four children, and several pets.